The Little Book of Storyboards

Boards for storytelling

**Written by
Jan Stringer**

Additional material and editing by Sally Featherstone

Illustrations by Martha Hardy

The Little Book of Storyboards
ISBN 1-905019-75-0 • 978-1-905019-75-5

© Featherstone Education Ltd, 2007
Text © Jan Stringer, 2007
Series Editor, Sally Featherstone

First published in the UK, March 2007

'Little Books' is a trade mark of Featherstone Education Ltd

Published in the United Kingdom by
Featherstone Education Ltd
44 - 46 High Street
Husbands Bosworth
Leicestershire
LE17 6LP

Printed in the UK on paper produced in the European Union from managed, sustainable forests

Contents

Introduction

Storyboards of all types have been used for a long time to display information such as pictures, words and symbols to many sorts of audiences. They convey information quickly and easily to a number of people simultaneously, so they are ideal for use in teaching.

Blackboards or chalkboards have been standard pieces of equipment in our classrooms for many years, as they allow information to be displayed quickly and changed easily to keep pace with verbal communication. In many schools and settings, traditional blackboards have been replaced by interactive whiteboards, making it much easier and quicker to add and remove information, and all in full colour!

Whiteboards boards can be used by a wide age and ability range, but participation by individual children can be limited as it is not easy for each child to take an active part when they are a member of a large class. It is also difficult to use tactile pieces on these boards as the glare from the board detracts from the pieces and the board tends to dominate the activity. Photographs of tactile characters could be included in stories but this process will obviously remove some of the tactile qualities!

Teachers and practitioners in many primary schools have made very good use of storyboards for displaying stories or sequences in a visual and appealing way. It was once a vital part of courses for most primary teachers at colleges when preparing for their teaching practice.

The storyboard allowed inexperienced teachers to prepare a session well in advance, to illustrate a story or concept, helping with the explanation or storytelling. Visual images are easier to remember than the written word and they allow a certain amount of interpretation by the individual listener. In a classroom situation they take the attention away from the teacher and onto the visual images on the storyboard, bringing the information to life. If the images are tactile, other senses are stimulated, helping to enhance concentration, memory and interpretation.

When tactile pieces are included, children can be involved in role play as the story progresses, and if there are a number of pieces more children can be involved, keeping the interest of all children and helping maintain interest and concentra-

tion within the group. Factual topics can also be depicted on storyboards, helping to explain new aspects and answer any questions from the children at the appropriate point, ensuring that delivery and detail of information is matched to the pace and nature of the group.

Using storyboards in groups or with whole classes helps with turn taking, sequencing and recognition of characters. A number of children can participate easily in the telling and retelling the story as children place and replace the pieces on the storyboard in turn. The storyboard can also be used with small groups or individuals to help develop story techniques or understand new concepts. Small group activities can also help children who are a bit unsure or shy in a larger group to make a contribution. Storyboards allow each child to participate in stories and other activities, where characters can be added by children as the story unfolds and their character appears. Characters can then be seen in the correct sequence, and the order can be followed as children add their characters and remove them as the story progresses. This is a very good way to develop listening skills and the concepts of stories.

Sharing stories on a one-to-one basis can help children with special needs to develop confidence and speech skills, and the same storyboard can be used to extend children with more advanced skills. If all of the children in the class have used the characters or pieces in the story, this will help with inclusion, as all will feel part of the same story.

Activities with storyboards can be a teacher led activity, or the storyboard and pieces can be left for small groups of children to use together. You will often observe children starting to retell the story among themselves, discussing the sequence of characters and possibly organising themselves into a role play group, taking on different characters. One group of children may develop a new story or extend a traditional tale, and could then tell this to other groups within the class or to other classes.

Basic storyboards, or those with simple back-grounds provide you and the children with a flexible resource for many stories, using traditional tales, picture book stories, or invented ones. Children and adults can add new characters and props to extend existing stories or link to other familiar tales.

As children become more used to how story-boards work, they can use the boards and the pieces to develop their own ideas before telling, drawing or writing a story. This will help them to put the story into a logical sequence, as it is easier to move the pieces on a storyboard to develop a story, and making the story with physical actions will reinforce the sequences they want to use. Given time and experience children will become skilled in using their imagination to develop complex structured stories in speech and writing, and may reach the stage where their imagination is sufficiently developed for them to stop using the visual clues offered by the boards.

Making Storyboards

Storyboards have been made in many different ways using a wide range of mate-rials over many years. The sections of this book look at a range of different types of storyboards and characters, starting with simple boards which are easy to make and develop using basic card, paper and other materials available in your setting or classroom. Of course, these simple boards will have a limited life, especially if used by a large number of children. Later sections of the book explore more durable boards with characters which can be used many times with a large number of children.

Most of the materials used are readily avail-able, but some may need to be obtained from specialist suppliers, and these are listed at the back of the book. Choose the type of board you feel comfortable with making, don't try to be too adventurous at first! Start simple and you will soon become more confident, imaginative and adventurous!

The Little Book of Storyboards

The characters and stories used in this book have been specially chosen to provide a range of ideas which can be used or easily adapted to other books and stories, building a range of useful resources. Some stories or concepts will have certain characters essential to the plot, so be selective in the stories you choose, as too many characters will make the board too crowded and it will be difficult to see clearly or use the board effectively. It will also be very time consuming making all the characters and situations and leave little to the imagination! It is ideal to make a background or a few backgrounds which can each be used with a number of stories, and don't put on too much detail, as this gives opportunities for children to add their own ideas in discussions and keeps the characters visually simple and easy to follow.

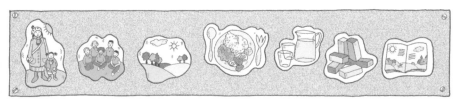

When you have chosen the characters and scenes, keep them a good size to use in a group or classroom situation and make sure they fit onto the board you are going to use. Characters also need to be in proportion to each other, although children don't seem to notice much if the aren't - and if you use a spider, such as Incy Wincy, then it needs to be big enough to see!

If you are choosing stories to make your first boards, remember to select ones with a few characters so that you can complete them in a reasonable amount of time and gain confidence using them in a class situation. As your confidence builds, produce or use more elaborate stories with more characters and scenes.

If you want to involve children in making some of the storyboards or characters, you could approach this in two ways. They could make the board and characters first and then see them used in the story, or know the story first and then make the board and characters to their own designs. Older children in the school may be able to help younger children make bits as part of their curriculum, as it would involve designing, preparation, cutting, sticking and imaginative skills to make the characters or the board.

Parents may like to be involved with making the boards and characters, particularly as this may involve them in offering their own craft skills. Some could help with the work at school if there is space and equipment, some might prefer to make their contribution at home, using their own tools and spaces. You may even be able to recruit some grandparents in your project.

In the selected stories and rhymes in this book, minimal characters and props are suggested, but many more can be added by you and the children to develop more detail or extend the story.

Keep the pieces for each story together in a bag, preferably with the book or story, and labelled for easy location and quick retrieval by you and by the children. Fabric or Ziplock bags are ideal for this, and you can add any notes or points about characters to the bag with the pieces to help you next time they are used.

You can make a single board with a simple background and use it for all the scenes in your story, or (like a film storyboard) you could have a range of different boards with different backgrounds for the locations of the story. This will allow you to move the characters from location to location and back again as the story unfolds. This might be useful for older children to help them develop imaginative and narrative skills.

Making and Using
the Storyboards

Card and Paper Storyboards
Modern Stories - The Hungry Caterpillar

This simple storyboard just needs card, some paint or felt pens and a bit of imagination.

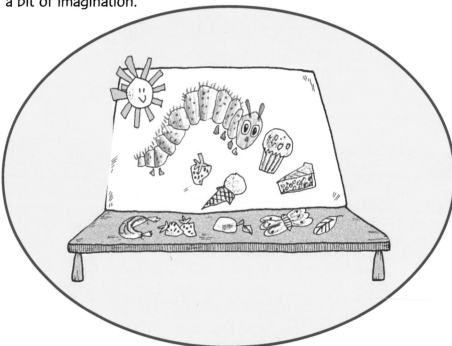

What you need:
* card for the board - the sides of a box would be ideal
* wool
* thin card, green paper
* string or wool
* a small box or container for the chrysalis
* fabric for the butterfly wings

Props and characters:
* a caterpillar (small)
* a caterpillar (larger)
* a butterfly
* a chrysalis that fits the butterfly
* 1 apple, 2 pears, 3plums, 4 strawberries, 5 oranges and the foods from the story

Making your board

1. This story only needs one board - a simple green painted board, perhaps with paper leaves stuck on it to make plants. Children could make this board with your help.
2. Cover the a big piece of strong card, such as the side of a big box, with paper and paint it green.
3. Cut some leaves from wrapping paper or foil paper, and stick them round the edge of the board.
4. Make two holes in the board so the little caterpillar can crawl through and the big caterpillar can crawl out again.
5. Make another hole in the board where you can hold the chrysalis, so the caterpillar can crawl into it from the back of the board and the butterfly can crawl out of the front (you may need to practice this!!).
6. Now let the children help to make the characters and props:
   * the small and larger caterpillars from card, coloured with felt pens or paint;
   * the butterfly (it would be good to make this from felt or fabric so you can fold it inside the chrysalis);
   * the chrysalis (from felt, fabric, foam or bubble wrap) with a flap for the caterpillar and butterfly;
   * the food that the caterpillar ate - leaves, fruit and other foods.

   If you are working with younger children, you may want to speed up the process by cutting the shapes out and letting the children colour and decorate them.
7. The characters in this story could be fixed to the board with Blutack or double sided tape.

Using your Hungry Caterpillar board

Prop the board up somewhere easy to see and reach. Now you could:

* tell the story yourself, moving the characters and props across the board as you go, and making the caterpillar move in and out of the holes in the board, eating the leaves the children have made. You will need to practice the chrysalis and butterfly bit so it looks convincing, and may need another pair of hands to help;

* work with your teaching assistant to share the book and the work with the board;

* let different children choose which prop they would like to use, adding them to the board at the right time in the story;

* use a book of the story and let the children manage the storyboard while you tell the story;

* leave the storyboards where children can play with them on their own, making up stories and retelling the ones they know.

and more ...

* Make slots at the top of the board to display the fruit for counting.
* Use a clear plastic bag opened out into a strip along the top of the board to display pages of the book, opened out.
* Use the board and the fruit for counting and sorting work.
* Have real fruits to look at, handle and taste.

Card and Paper Storyboards
Traditional Stories - Goldilocks

This simple storyboard just needs card, some paint and a bit of imagination.

What you need:
* pieces of card for the board - the sides of a box would be ideal
* card for the characters and props - cereal box card would be fine
* paint

Props and characters:
* Goldilocks
* Daddy, Mummy & Baby Bear
* three bowls
* three spoons
* three chairs
* three beds
(you could get the children to draw these or cut them out from a catalogue)

Making your board

1. Cut three pieces of card the same size. They will be the three scenes for your story - the house front with an open door; the kitchen with a table for the three bowls, spoons and chairs; the bedroom for the three beds.

2. Draw the three scenes:
   * the bears' house with windows and a simple opening door (make a card door and put tape down the hinge side so it will open when Goldilocks comes to call);
   * the kitchen just needs a window and room for the table and the three chairs;
   * the bedroom with enough room for the beds and the sleeping bears.

3. Now carefully make slits in the backgrounds for the characters and props. You need:
   * three slits outside the door for the bears;
   * one in the kitchen floor for Goldilocks, three on the table for the bowls, three for the chairs;
   * three in the bedroom for the beds, and three for the bears when they come back.

4. Colour the scenes with paint or felt pens.

5. Draw the chairs, beds, spoons, bowls, bears and Goldilocks on thinner card, or cut them from a mail order catalogue and stick them on card. If you want to be really clever, cut some fabric covers for the beds and stick them on.

6. Now you are ready to tell the story.

Using your Goldilocks board

Now you have the three boards, telling the story will be easy.
Prop the three boards up somewhere easy to see and reach.
Now you could:

* tell the story yourself, slotting the characters and props into the slots as you go, and moving the characters from board to board as the scene changes;

* work with your teaching assistant to share the telling and the work with the board;

* give each character to a different child, so they can add them to the board and take them off again as the story progresses;

* let different children choose which characters to be, and speak for them at the appropriate time in the story;

* use a book of the story and let the children manage the story board while you tell the story;

* leave the storyboards where children can play with them on their own, making up stories and retelling the ones they know.

and more ...

* Make full and empty bowls.
* Let the children make more props and characters (don't worry if they are not to scale!). They could make trees and animals for the forest, Goldilocks' house and family, fences and gates etc.

Card and Paper Storyboards
Nursery Rhyme - Mary, Mary

This storyboard helps with counting and nursery rhymes.

What you need:
- card for the board - the sides of a box would be ideal
- paint or felt pens
- paper

Props and characters:
- thin card for flowers, shells and bells and numbers
- foil for bells
- card for a picture of Mary

Making your Nursery Rhyme board

1. The board is a simple piece of sturdy card, covered with paper and painted.
2. The bells, shells and flowers are made so they flap down as children sing the song and count to five.
3. Cut three strips of card the same width as your storyboard.
4. Fold each piece in half lengthwise and cut to the fold to make five flaps in each strip (see diagram).

5. Now flatten the strips out and turn them into strips of five bells, five shells and five flowers by:
   * sticking foil bells on one strip;
   * making five shell pictures on the second strip;
   * drawing five flowers on the third strip.
6. Stick the thin part of each strip on the storyboard so the objects are hidden until the flaps are turned down (see diagram).

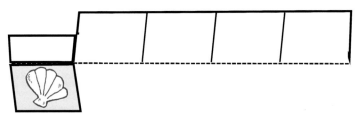

7. Check to make sure the picture flaps don't get in each other's way!
8. Make a card figure of Mary. You could use a magazine picture or get the children to make it and stick it on card. Put Mary in the garden.

Using your 'Mary, Mary Quite Contrary' board

Now you have the board, telling the story will be easy. Prop the board up somewhere easy to see and reach. Now you could:

* sing the rhyme together, flapping the bells, shells and flowers down as you sing;

* work with your teaching assistant to help with the flaps and the counting of each strip;

* let the children sing, and pause in the song to count the objects;

> Mary, Mary, quite contrary,
> How does your garden grow?
> With silver bells' *(one, two, three, four, five)*
> And cockle shells' *(one, two, three, four, five)*
> And pretty maids all in a row, row, row'
> And pretty maids all in a row' *(one, two, three, four, five)*
> *(Pretty Maids are flowers!)*

* leave the storyboard where children can play with it on their own, making up songs and rhymes as well as practising the ones they know.

and more ...

* Write the numbers 1-5 on each row of flaps to encourage number recognition.
* Make some number cards and attach them with Blutack to the board under each row of pictures.
* Grow some seeds in pots and put them near the storyboard so they can grow into a frame for your work.
* Make more counting strips for other simple number rhymes.

MDF Storyboards

MDF (medium density fibre-board) is a cheap strong board made from compressed sawdust. It comes in big sheets, enough to make six or eight storyboards, but it's quite hard to cut, so ask a DIY store to cut it to size for you. An ideal size is 45cm x 60cm, but any size is possible.

You can fix a large board to the back of a door or the wall in your classroom or setting, at a height suitable for children to use easily. Put some pockets, bags or baskets of story items nearby, with the book they relate to.

Smaller boards can be:
* propped against a wall, chair or easel (make sure they don't slide forward);
* made into an A frame to stand on their own (hinge them at the tops and put two screws and a bit of string halfway down each side to stop them collapsing);
* placed on a big book stand;
* hung from a strong hook in the wall in a suitable area such as a story corner (make two holes at the top of the board and thread a cord through);
* used flat on a table or on the floor.

Prepare your basic board by cleaning off any dust from cutting with a damp cloth. The board could by left as its own colour but would be better if treated in one of the following ways;
* draw scenes with big felt pens;
* paint the board one colour using primer to seal the surface then use emulsion paint from 'test pots' (a cheap way to get lots of colours);
* you could paint sky and land in blue and green shades, or land and water to suit the stories you like to use. Seal the board first with primer or undercoat;
* paint one scene on the front and a different one on the back of the board - add details could be added using paint or felt pens;
* stick card shapes onto the scene with strong glue;
* use Blutack to add details to a painted board, to allow them to be moved or changed easily for different stories.

MDF boards are more robust for classroom use and once you have made this sort of board it will last a long time, and can be used many times. The paint may chip but if you keep the spare paint you can easily and quickly do running repairs. You may consider making a bag or cover to protect the board when not in use.

Characters, props and other objects can be attached to this type of board with Blutack, double sided tape to allow them to be moved around easily. Take care if using Blutack with under threes it Blutack can easily be swallowed.

Velcro - dots can be used if they are attached at suitable points on the scene and the connecting dot stuck on back of the pieces. This restricts the positions of the characters and could be frustrating for younger children who don't understand how to position or link up the pieces, but it would develop good hand/eye coordination. Black and white dots are widely available but will be visible on the actual scene where no pieces are attached. If you use the board flat on a table or the floor, you will not need Blutack or Velcro. The pieces can be moved around freely by the teacher or the children.

The Little Book of Storyboards

MDF Storyboards
Traditional Story - Little Red Riding Hood

A simple story for your new MDF storyboard.

What you need:
- a double sided MDF storyboard
- paper and paint or felt pens to make a background scene for the story
- card for figures
- fabric scraps, wool

Props and characters:
- Little Red Riding Hood
- the wolf without clothes
- the wolf (in Grandmother's clothes)
- Grandmother
- the woodcutter
- a basket
- a bunch of flowers
- Grandmother's bed
- trees and flowers for the forest
- velcro dots

Making your storyboard

1. Paint the front of the board green for grass and blue for sky. Then paint the back with walls and floor for the inside of Grandmother's house.

2. Now make some trees and flowers from paper, card or fabric for the forest, and stick them on the board with Blutack or double sided tape. Make sure one tree is very near the edge of the board, so the wolf can hide behind it!

3. Make the characters from good quality card, so they last longer. You can make them yourself or let the children help, making clothes from fabric scraps, hair from wool etc.

4. Laminate the finished characters to make them last longer, if you like, and stick Velcro dots or Blutack on each one.

5. Cut out a bed for Grandmother, with a long cover so she can hide under the bed if you don't want the wolf to eat her! Make a basket for Red Riding Hood. Colour them and add Blutack.

6. Now you are ready to tell Red Riding Hood's story.

7. Before you start, put Grandmother in her bed on the back of the board, so she is ready for the wolf to arrive, and have the wolf dressed as Grandmother ready to slot into the bed at the right time.

8. On the front of the board, make the forest with the trees and flowers, and add Red Riding Hood and her basket. Now she can 'walk' from one side of the forest to the other, meeting the wolf on the way. Tuck the wolf figure behind one of the trees so he can come out to meet her.

9. As Red Riding Hood leaves the forest, turn the board over to show the house, and tell the next part of the story before she comes into the bedroom.

10. You will need to decide how the story ends, and how Grandmother is rescued!

MDF Storyboards

Modern Stories - The Bad Tempered Ladybird

Another story for your new MDF storyboard.

What you need:
* an MDF storyboard
* paper, paint or felt pens to make a background scene for the story; card for figures
* velcro dots

Props and characters:
* 2 ladybirds
* a wasp
* a stag beetle
* a praying mantis
* a sparrow
* a lobster
* a skunk
* a boa constrictor
* a hyena
* a gorilla
* a rhinoceros
* an elephant
* a whale

Copy or trace the creatures from a book, or trace them, then enlarge them on a photocopier

Making your storyboard

1. Let the children help you make the background for the story. You could paint it on a sheet of paper or card, or direct on the MDF board. You could use both sides of the storyboard, - one for the sea and one for the land, turning the board as the ladybird's adventure moves from land to sea to land again.

2. You could make the characters yourself, so you keep the proportions of the creatures right, or let the children help - they will really enjoy this, even though the sizes and shapes of the finished articles may not be perfect!

3. Laminate the finished creatures to make them last longer, and stick Velcro dots or Blutack on each one.

4. Cut some props from card and colour or paint them. You need:
   > a leaf with aphids on it
   > a leaf with no aphids
   > a simple clock face with moving hands, or an actual clock.

5. Fix the clock face on the board so the children can follow the time changing as the story progresses.

6. Now you are ready to tell the story, moving the hands of the clock as you go. This is a complicated story, so tell it several times with the children helping, moving the characters on and off the board before you use it to explore other ideas.

and more ...

* Count and order the characters, either by size or by their place in the story.

* Add the sun, moon and stars and explore day and night before talking about the times of day in the story. Younger children may not be ready for this, so use your judgement in deciding how complex to make the activity.

MDF Storyboards
Nursery Rhyme - Little Miss Muffet

This rhyme has a moveable spider that can come down to frighten Miss Muffet.

What you need:
- an MDF storyboard
- paper and paint or felt pens to make a background scene for the story
- card for figures
- fabric for Miss Muffet's clothes
- pipe cleaners, wool or thin elastic, black fabric or a black sock for the spider

Props and characters:
- Miss Muffet
- the spider
- a bowl
- a stool
- a tree
- velcro dots

Copy or trace the creatures from a book, or trace them, then enlarge them on a photocopier

Making and using your storyboard

1. The board just needs sky and grass. You could paint a tree or make one from card with green paper leaves.
2. The two characters in this rhyme can be quite big. Help the children to make them by stuffing a piece of fabric or a sock with paper and tying it closed with wool. Add googly eyes and pipe cleaner legs. Then tie on a piece of wool or thin elastic so he can be lowered from the tree.
3. Miss Muffet is a card figure, with clothes made from fabric scraps, with wool for hair etc.
4. Cut the props (a bowl, spoon, stool) and a tree from card and decorate with crayons, felt pens or paint out.
5. Add Velcro dots or Blutack to the characters and props.
6. If you work with older children, it would be good to have the rhyme written on a big sheet of card or paper for the children to follow.
7. Make a loop in the end of the spider's string so you can lower him over the top of the board so he looks as if he is coming down from the tree as you say the rhyme.
8. Once you have learned the rhyme together, leave the board and characters for the children to use independently.

and more ...

* This is a good way to help children overcome a fear of spiders by making them familiar characters and fun to use.
* Use the board to tell other simple stories and rhymes by adding characters made by the children.
* let the children make figures of themselves and tell stories or make up rhymes about the children in your class.

Felt Storyboards

Felt storyboards (such as Fuzzy Felts) have been produced by toy and game makers for years, and many become favourites at home and school. The board is usually smaller and lighter, and is used at an angle, or flat on the table to keep the pieces in place. Keeping the board flatter is a small price to pay for the added flexibility of this sort of board.

You need:
* a piece of MDF or thick card for the backing;
* a piece of felt, big enough to cover the board, and ideally to fold over the edges; this stops the felt from peeling off the backing *(a neutral colour such a beige, pale blue or pale green will be the most versatile);*
* white glue or fabric glue such as Copydex *(You could just staple the edges of the felt to the back of the board, pulling the felt tight so the surface of the front is smooth, but felt does stretch and the surface may become baggy over time).*

and for the characters and props, you need:
* felt in different colours, fine felt pens, stick-on eyes (optional).
* sharp scissors

Draw the characters and props on the felt, then cut them out and draw, stick or sew features and details on each. Use bright colours to provide a good contrast with the background, and don't make the figures too heavy, or they will fall off!

If you make the board big enough, the children may like to help with making the figures. However, smaller figures may be a bit fiddly for them to make, and the felt needs sharp scissors, but children will love using the ones you make.

Felt Storyboards
Traditional Story - The Billy Goats Gruff

A good starter for a felt board.

What you need:
* a felt storyboard
* felt for the characters, the sun etc
* blue fabric for the river
* card for the bridge

Props and characters:
* the three goats
* the river
* the bridge
* the troll

If you are not a confident artist, copy or trace the goats and the troll from a book, then enlarge them on a photocopier.

If you make a sun and some clouds from felt, you can use them for lots of stories.

Making and using your storyboard

1. The goats and the troll need some careful cutting with sharp scissors. They also need to be clearly different sizes, so the children can differentiate between them. Draw features with a fine felt pen, and make some clothes for the troll from scraps of fabric or felt, stuck on to the felt body.

2. Choose a piece of blue fabric for the river, and lay it across the board from one side to the other. Staple or tape the ends to the back of the board to keep it in place. Leave room on each side of the bridge for a field.

3. Draw the bridge on card and cut it out. Fix the two ends of the bridge to the board, but leave the middle loose, so the goats can run over it and the troll can hide underneath.

4. Put all three goats in one field and you are ready to tell the story.

5. Don't forget to leave the storyboard where children can return to it in their own time, retelling the story in their own way.

and more ...

* Use the goats for comparing sizes and for counting.
* Make a few more goats and play 'One more, one less'.
* Talk about position, using 'over', 'under', 'through', 'first', 'second', 'third', 'last'.
* Don't forget that children love to retell stories in action - be the Billy Goats Gruff in your garden, with a chalk river and a plank for the bridge.
* Use the board for other stories about three - Three Bears, Three Pigs.
* Help the children to make up a new version about Five Billy Goats Gruff.

Felt Storyboards
Modern Picture Book - The Owl Babies

This favourite story makes a good felt storyboard subject.

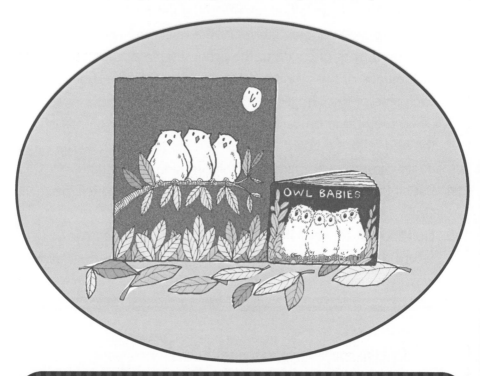

What you need:
* a felt storyboard
* felt for the characters and the scene

Props and characters:
* the three owl babies
* the mother owl
* the branch
* the moon
* the sun
* the owls' nest

If you are not a very confident artist, copy or trace the characters from a book, or get the children to draw them on paper and use these as templates.

Making and using your storyboard

1. The baby owls will need to be double sided, one side awake, the other side asleep. Make them from light coloured felt and add open eyes on one side, closed on the other. Add feather marks, beaks and claws on both sides, using felt pens. You could make separate little wings for the babies and stick them on the bodies for a more realistic shape.

2. The mother owl needs to be a darker colour. Make her with open wings and fold these for the bits of the story when she isn't flying. Add face and feather details to her too.

3. You will also need a brown nest and a brown tree branch.

4. The children could help to make leaves for the trees, as these can be more approximate shapes.

5. Make a yellow sun and a white or silver moon.

6. Now you are ready to tell the story, placing the props and characters on the board and moving the baby owls in and out of the nest according to the time of day or night in the story. You could easily involve the children in this story by letting them move the characters and props while you tell the story. this is a great activity for a small group.

and more ...

* Use the story to prompt discussions about day and night, mothers and babies, feeling lonely, brothers and sisters.

* Make a different family of birds and use them to create a new story.

* Use the board to make a story about nocturnal animals, by adding a fox, a badger, a cat, a mouse.

* Make up more stories about being lost or frightened, including real experiences from the children. Use some figures of the children in the group.

Felt Storyboards
Number Rhymes - Ten Green Bottles

Now try a counting rhyme!

What you need:
- a felt storyboard
- felt for the bottles
- white stickers or white felt
- a piece of red fabric
- a black felt pen

Props and characters:
- the ten bottles
- the wall

Children could find or draw pictures of bottles, cut them out and stick them on felt (use thin paper so they are not too heavy)

Making and using your storyboard

1. Stretch the red fabric over the bottom half of the board and fix it at the back with staple, strong glue or tape.
2. Now use the felt pen to make a brick pattern on the wall.
3. Make ten bottles from green felt, and stick a numbered label on each, using squares of felt or stickers.
4. You could decorate the base of the wall with flowers if you like.
5. Put the bottles on the wall before you start singing.
6. You may want to change the words of the song a bit to say 'Ten green bottles standing on the wall' but the children probably won't mind if you don't!
7. As you sing, remove the bottles in turn and stand them in order along the bottom of the wall.

and more ...

This board is great for all sorts of counting rhymes and activities:

* Make seasonal versions - ten brown leaves, ten yellow daffodils, ten seaside buckets, ten little snowmen.
* Use it to practice and reinforce 'one more' and 'one less'.
* Make other figures to use while singing your own versions of favourite nursery songs and rhymes 'Ten in the Bed', 'Ten Brown Buns', 'Ten Little Ducks', 'Ten Fast Cars'.
* Leave the storyboard in the maths area for children to play with in their own way. Encourage them to make up their own stories and songs about five or ten.
* Older children could use the board for simple addition and subtraction problems.
* Make some more bottles and use the board with older children for work up to 20.

Felt Storyboards
Nursery Rhyme - Humpty Dumpty

A simple rhyme for younger children that will become a firm favourite for independent play.

What you need:
* a felt storyboard
* felt for the characters, the sun etc
* red fabric for the wall
* felt pens

Props and characters:
* Humpty Dumpty (whole)
* Humpty Dumpty (in pieces)
* the King's men (on horses)

Horses are hard to draw, use a book to help you. Once you have done one, photocopy it till you have plenty!
If you have made a wall for ten Green Bottles you could use it again for this rhyme.

Health & Safety
Children should not handle raw eggs or egg shells. Make sure that eggs are cooked until the yolk and white are hard.

Making and using your storyboard

1. If you haven't already made a felt board wall, stretch a piece of red fabric across the board and then mark it with lines for bricks.

2. Make the two Humpty Dumpty figures from felt - the oval body shape is easy, then just make legs and arms to attach, and cover these and the bottom half of the body with some suitable fabric for trousers. Add some boots or shoes. The broken Humpty Dumpty figure can just be the pieces.

3. The soldiers on the horses are more difficult, but draw one on card and use this as a template, or photocopy it and stick each one onto felt. You can make as many as you like - even enough for every child to have one, even though you may have to overlap them on the board.

4. Put the whole Humpty Dumpty on top of the wall and you are ready to tell the story.

5. You could write out the rhyme, so the children can follow the words.

6. Now have fun saying the rhyme and moving the characters. Some quick action is needed to change the whole Humpty Dumpty for the pieces.

and more ...

* Play out the rhyme with the children as the King's men.
* Look at other jigsaws and talk about how the pieces fit together. Make some from old greetings card.
* Use the soldiers to make a new story - how about The Grand Old Duke of York?
* Hard boil some eggs and decorate them with faces. Look carefully at the shells when you break them to eat the eggs.
* Talk about happy and sad faces and other expressions.

Magnetic Storyboards

There are lots of different magnetic boards available for setting and classroom use, either as a fixture on the wall, or as smaller portable boards. Most of them are white, with a smooth, shiny surface, which has advantages and disadvantages.

If you want to make a magnetic board yourself, you can buy magnetic paint (see resources section at the end of the book). This is a special type of paint for covering whole walls. Two coats are required, and once they have dried, the area can be painted with normal coloured paint, producing a magnetic wall where pieces can be attached and removed easily from the coloured surface. You could paint a piece of MDF with this magnetic paint after it has been sealed with primer to produce a portable coloured magnetic area.

Small self adhesive magnets or pieces of magnetic strip can be placed behind characters or scenery. Some craft shops supply sheets of magnetic paper to draw on or use in a computer printer.

Pieces can be added and removed easily as a story develops, but some boards do not hold pieces as well as others, so check this as larger pieces may fall easily and spoil the flow of your story.

Think carefully before positioning a magnetic board or painting a wall. If you use a painted wall for stories you will need it to be high enough to be accessible for adults and low enough for children to use too, so they can reach to help you with the story and retell stories themselves.

Magnetic Storyboards
Traditional Story - Jack and the Beanstalk

This is a great use for a magnetic wall!

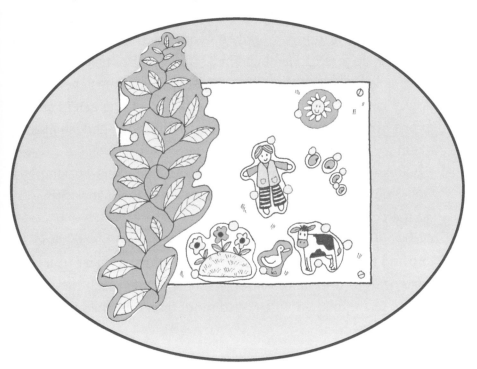

What you need:
- a magnetic storyboard or wall
- strong card for the characters
- fabric and wool for clothes and hair
- green fabric for the beanstalk leaves and some green cord

Props and characters:
- Jack
- Jack's mother
- the giant
- the cow
- the beanstalk
- Jack's axe
- the hen and golden eggs
- the giant's wife (optional)

Adjust the characters according to the version of the story you know. You can add the golden harp, clouds, coins, five beans, the giant's wife etc.

Making and using your storyboard

1. Children could cut the leaves from fabric, and then you could fasten them to a piece of cord. Fix the bottom end to the frame of your board, then screw a cup hook in the top of the board so you can make the beanstalk grow by pulling the cord upwards through the hook.

2. Make the giant from strong card - you may need to make him in pieces so you can laminate him. You can also make him pose-able if you join the bits together with paper fasteners!

3. Make Jack, his mother, the cow and the other characters and props from card, adding fabric, wool, buttons etc, and laminate them for strength and durability.

4. Stick magnetic strip on all the props and characters, making sure you have enough bits on each to make them stick firmly to the board.

5. Now tell the story, letting the children help by attaching and moving the characters and props as the story unfolds. You may need to offer a low stool, so children can reach the top of the board, and you may need more than one child to operate the giant!

and more ...

* Give the children free access to the story pieces so they can reinforce the sequence of the story by retelling it themselves.
* Draw round children for the outline of the giant and the giant's wife.
* Use the beanstalk as a vertical number line with numbers on each leaf. Then the children can count as Jack goes up and down and the giant follows him.
* Plant some beans near the board for a real beanstalk story.

The Little Book of Storyboards

Magnetic Storyboards
Modern Picture Book - The Great Pet Sale

Involve lots of children in this favourite animal story.

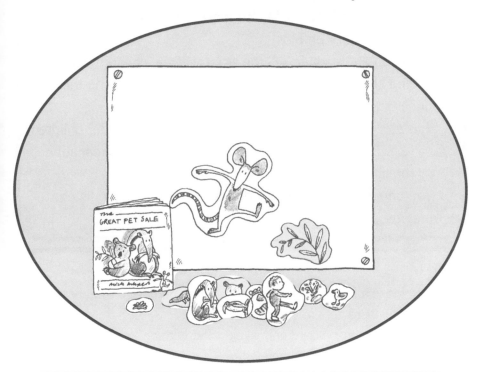

What you need:
- a magnetic storyboard or wall
- strong card for the characters

Props and characters:
- tortoise
- pelican, puffin, penguin, parrot, platypus
- salamander
- skink
- gecko
- koala, ant eater
- box of little brown creatures
- Komodo dragon in a box
- rat
- price tags

The animals in this story are hard to draw if you don't have the book. Just a thought! - this story is worth the cost of buying a copy of the book and cutting it up!

Making and using your storyboard

1. Either draw the characters on card or cut them out from the book. Laminating them will make them more durable.
2. Attach a magnet to the back of each.
3. Make the price tags, add wool or string and loop them onto the characters. You could also make some 'SOLD' signs to add as the story unfolds.
4. Now you are ready to tell the story. Let the children help by adding characters as they appear in the story, putting the price tags on or adding 'SOLD' labels.
5. This story has quite a complicated sequence, so older children can be given a more challenging role in listening, repeating or retelling it.
6. You could record the story on tape so children can listen to it as they manipulate the characters.

and more ...

* Make a big picture of the story on a long piece of paper with the characters in the right order.
* Make a storyboard animal alphabet with an animal, bird or other creature for each letter.
* Use the pets for counting, recognition, sorting by size or kind, tails and no tails, colour, habitat etc.
* Use the story to talk about money, and maybe make a pet shop in your setting, with soft toys or small world pets.
* Visit a pet shop or ask a vet to visit to talk about pet care.
* Make pictures and collections of the children's own pets or the pet they would choose if they could.
* Talk about what each animal eats and how they would care for it if they took it to their house. Discuss exercise, space and company as well as just food.

Magnetic Storyboards
Number Rhymes - Ten Fat Sausages

A good starter for a magnetic board.

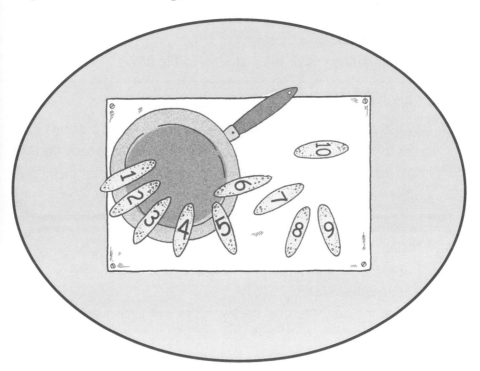

What you need:
* a magnetic storyboard or wall
* strong card for the props
* felt pens

Props:
* a big frying pan shape
* ten sausages
* number cards 1-10

This rhyme is one of many that you can use to help the children with number recognition and counting. Be inventive! You don't have to be an artist to make games that the children will love and will play with for hours.

Making and using your storyboard

1. Make the pan in thin card. You could use the inside of a tough plastic carrier, the plastic will be lighter and easier to attach, but you will need to use permanent markers to colour it.

2. Now make ten fat sausages from tough card and laminate them if possible. You could start with five for younger children. Children could make these!

3. Add some magnets or magnet strip to the props.

4. If the pan is too thick for the magnets to work, make some slots in the pan and slot the sausages in.

5. Say the rhyme, removing sausages as you go, and putting them in front of the board. When the children are ready you could add some number cards to the rhyme, or write them on the sausages.

and more ...

* Let the children make more sausages and continue the rhyme beyond ten.

* Use the game to count backwards as well as forwards or to reinforce 'one more' and 'one less'.

* Older children will enjoy other versions of the game - two sausages could go 'BANG' each time, or you could choose different numbers every time, for encouraging quick thinking.

* In a small group, children could have a paper plate each to collect the sausages as the rhyme goes on.

* You could make some really fat sausages from the fingers of gloves, stuffed with paper or cotton wool and fastened with elastic bands. Or you could make a really huge set from the legs of tights, stuffed with newspaper, draw a big pan on the ground outside and play the game in the garden or on the floor inside.

Velcro® Storyboards

These boards are covered in Velcro receptive fabric and can be made yourself or obtained from various suppliers. More elaborate boards can be made by sewing different coloured pieces of the fabric together or they can be purchased ready made from a few select suppliers. Ready made boards are usually supplied in one colour but some suppliers have or can make them in a range of colours.

If you want to make your own board, you can buy the Velcro® fabric with or without a foam backing, and with or without a self adhesive backing. The fabric can be stuck onto the board or sewn into a 'bag' to slip onto the board to cover it. Remember, the self adhesive fabric is only available in a very limited range of colours and from a very limited range of stockists.

Fabric with a foam backing can be glued onto a board with a PVA glue, the fabric without a foam back will not have as good a finish if it is glued to the board. Attach the fabric to a piece of MDF or other type of board cut to size or attached to an area of wall. Put a wooden frame round the edge or bind it with duct or carpet tape to stop the fabric peeling off at the edges.

You could cover a large board and attach it to a wall or to the back of a cupboard for children to use.

Smaller boards can be:
* made into an A frame to be free standing on a table
* made as a flat board and propped against a wall
* propped against the back of a chair
* placed on a flat surface such as a table or carpet area.

The fabric boards can be cleaned with a damp cloth if they are fixed. If they are loose covers they can be removed and washed.

Velcro® fabric boards are very durable and can be used for many classroom activities. Pieces can be made of:
* card or laminated card
* felts
* fabrics
* plastic with writing in dry wipe markers
* magazine pictures etc.

The hook side of Velcro® can be sewn or stuck in place on the back of the pieces.

Velcro® Storyboards
Traditional Story - The Three Little Pigs

A good starter for a Velcro® board.

What you need:
* a Velcro® storyboard
* Velcro® strip or dots
* felt, fabric or plastic for characters
* felt pens

Props and characters:
* thee pigs
* the wolf
* the pigs' houses

Use felt, fabric or plastic for the figures. The back of tough carrier bags is really good, easy to cut and smooth to draw on. You need permanent markers for drawing on this plastic.

Making and using your storyboard

1. The ideal board for this story is blue at the top and green at the bottom, but don't worry if it isn't.
2. Make the pigs (pink plastic or felt) and the wolf (grey plastic or fur fabric), and add Velcro® strip or dots to the back of each one.
3. Make the houses for the pigs by drawing them and sticking straw on one and twigs on the second. Colour the third one red and draw brick marks on it. You could make little doors and windows that open if you like.
4. Now make a fireplace to complete the props.
5. Stick Velcro® strip on all the props and characters, making sure you have enough bits on each to make them stick firmly to the board.
6. Now tell the story, letting the children help by attaching and moving the characters and props as the story unfolds. Removing the pieces takes a bit of practice because some stick really firmly and take a bit of gentle persuasion.

and more ...

* Label the houses and the pigs and use for counting and number recognition.
* Talk about different building materials and their strength and durability.
* Try making some houses and testing them in the wind and rain outside.
* Use Lego to explore building walls, trying different ways of fixing the bricks in different patterns.
* Collect some sticks and twigs in the garden or park and use these to make houses, dens and shelters.

Velcro® Storyboards
Modern Picture Book - Handa's Surprise

A firm favourite which is ideal for this sort of board.

What you need:
* a Velcro storyboard
* Velcro strip or dots
* felt, fabric or plastic for characters
* felt pens

Props and characters:
* Handa
* Handa's friend
* the fruits
* the animals' heads

Use felt, fabric or plastic for the figures. The back of tough carrier bags is really good, easy to cut and smooth to draw on. You need permanent markers for drawing on this plastic.

Making and using your storyboard

1. The pieces for this story need to be really hardwearing because you and the children will use it again and again. If you are good at sewing, try sewing the Handa figure and the animal heads, using the book to help you. Otherwise, make the characters and props from card or felt with Velcro® tabs or dots on the back.

2. As well as Handa, her friend and her big basket, you need:

Fruit	Animal heads
a pineapple	a monkey
an avocado	an ostrich
a passion fruit	a zebra
a red mango	an elephant
a banana	a giraffe
a guava	an antelope
an orange	a parrot
10 tangerines	a goat

The children could help with these.

3. When you have made all these, let the children choose which fruit or animal they will add, and begin the story, starting by putting all the fruit (except the tangerines) in the basket, and gradually taking them out as the animals appear.

and more ...

* Download some pictures of the real fruit from Google and print them for a different set.
* Get some jungle finger puppets and use these, by attaching some Velcro® to the back of each.
* Prop the board up so the animal heads can appear over the top of the board as they take their favourite fruit. Using finger puppets or glove puppets for this version is very good fun, which the children will love!

Velcro® Storyboards
Nursery Rhyme - Old MacDonald's Farm

More animals and people in this familiar rhyming song.

What you need:
* a Velcro® storyboard
* Velcro® strip or dots
* felt, fabric or plastic for the characters
* felt pens

Props and characters:
* Old MacDonald
* cow
* pig
* sheep
* horse
* dog
* duck and any others you fancy!

This is a good opportunity to use patterned and textured fabrics - fur, stripes, spots, velvets etc. If you enjoy sewing, you can neaten the edges or even hem them to prevent fraying.

Making and using your storyboard

1. You can make the animal characters from photos, download pictures from the Internet or copy some from books. You could use finger puppets or print some on special Velcro® picture paper (see Resources page at the end of the book). You can have as many animals as you like, you don't have to use them all every time, and they will be useful for other stories.
2. Make Old MacDonald and attach him to the edge of the story-board, so he can see what is going on as all the animals gather. You could make him a farmhouse or a gate to lean on.
3. Decide which order you are going to sing the verses and let the children choose which animals they will use and when.
4. Now you are ready to sing!
5. Add the animals to the board, and they will help the children to remember the order of the sounds they need to make.

and more ...

* Make some speech bubbles for the animals and place each one near the right animal's mouth.
* Add more animals when children suggest them by writing their names and drawing their pictures on bits of card.
* Children can put all the animals on the board and take them off one by one, making the right sound each time.
* Use birds, jungle animals, cold land animals, even dinosaurs for a change - and change the farmer.
* Make duplicates of some animals, add a Noah's ark picture and sing 'The Animals went in Two by Two'.
* Make stories about mother and baby animals, animal families, night time animals, the seaside, underwater etc.
* Use the set for other animal stories such as 'I Went to the Animal Fair', Elmer the Patchwork Elephant', 'Rumble in the Jungle'.

Velcro® Storyboards

Number Rhymes - Five Little Ducks

Good for 'one more, one less'!

What you need:
* a Velcro® storyboard
* Velcro® strip or dots
* felt or fabric for characters
* felt pens
* some blue fabric

Props and characters:
* Mother duck
* five baby ducks
* flowers, trees, sun etc.

This story uses simple props and characters, easy to draw and reproduce, even for the most inexperienced or modest practitioner!

Making and using your storyboard

1. This is another story that ideally needs blue at the top and green at the bottom, but don't worry if it isn't, you can just fix a strip of fabric or card across the middle to make the stream, and add some flowers and trees.
2. Make the mother duck and the five baby ducks from strong card - download some images or copy some from a book. Laminating them will make them even tougher.
3. Stick Velcro® strips or dots on the back of each (put it at the top of their backs so they can stick above the fabric stream.
4. You can add a pond with some reeds, or clouds and a sun if you wish to make the scene more interesting.
5. Sing or say the rhyme as the ducks swim away one at a time, disappearing behind the board and finally appearing again as the song ends
6. Even very small children will be able to join in and follow this simple appearing and disappearing rhyme.

and more ...

* Number the ducks so you can use them for counting on, back, one more, one less.
* Add more ducks for number work from 0 to 10.
* Use the same board for 'Five Little Speckled Frogs', 'One, Two, Three, Four, Five' and other rhymes, including some you make up yourself to familiar tunes.
* Tell some more duck stories - Farmer Duck, Fix-it Duck, Duck's Day Out, Duck in a Truck, Daisy to the Rescue.
* Get some yellow bath ducks for water play and use them for counting and sorting as well as for games. If you write numbers on them, you can use them for all sorts of number games. Try them in a paddling pool outside, with nets.

Additional Storyboard Ideas

There are hundreds of ways of using and exploiting the storyboard experience. It is a powerful learning and teaching method and engages all sorts of learners - visual, auditory and kinesthetic. This fact alone should be sufficient to convince practitioners and their managers to embrace what is sometimes seen as an old-fashioned tool.

The book has hundreds of ideas for making and using storyboards for stories and rhymes, but they are also very valuable in lots of other ways that there was no room to explore in detail in one Little Book. These uses are wide ranging and we did not want to ignore them entirely, so here are some of the many ways in which you could use the boards in other areas and aspects of the curriculum. They may also convince others in your setting or school of the value of practical story telling and the place it should have in every child's education.

* In any stories, look for other characters you could use, especially if they can be drawn, printed or made easily.
* Remember that using different types of boards will suit different stories. The size and style depends on the story to be illustrated, the size of the class or group, the age and ability. be flexible and make more than one sort!

* Keep copies of patterns and information to replace parts.
* Once boards and characters have been made or purchased then make full use of them for other areas of the curriculum, not just for the stories. Choose stories which can easily be extended and developed to include other areas of the curriculum.

* Let children introduce additional characters and tell their story. Make these new characters or let children make them, then write down the new story for future reference.

* Take some of the characters and props from the story and use them for counting, to develop adding and taking away.
* If there are a large number of pieces let a group of children develop their own ways of sharing them fairly.
* Some stories lend themselves to portions and fractions. Use this in the story work to reinforce the concepts. A cake can be cut up into fractions if relevant in the story.
* A lot of stories offer opportunities to discuss relationships, both good and frightening ones. Use a story to move into discussions about feelings and relationships.
* Sometimes characters, such as Goldilocks and Red Riding Hood, go off on their own. Use these stories to discuss dangers of going into other people's houses and meeting strangers.
* Plans of and journeys through forests and scenes can be used to explore directions and develop some early map reading skills.
* Children are often inspired to write, draw, or make models in response to stories told with storyboards. This work can be displayed in the classroom with pieces from the storyboards.

* Older children can develop new skills of making and building if they are given a story to make a storyboard for and then tell the story to the rest of the class in groups or to individual children.
* Making and printing illustrations and labels for stories, using basic computer skills, offers ICT experience.

* Preparation is quick and easy for a basic board, but the more robust and durable boards that you can use in your setting over many years need to be able to stand wear and tear. Characters and props may need to be replaced because favourites may wear out or go on a walkabout!
* Storyboards can be used at all age and ability levels from early years, in the Foundation Stage, and through KS1 and even at KS2, 3 and 4. Don't forget that children with additional needs and those with EAL can really benefit from this approach at all levels.

The new Velcro picture paper allows you to print pictures quickly from the computer and when cut or coloured, needs no laminating!

* Use pieces to retell a story at the time and use again several weeks later with the same group as a reminder, a recap or a check on memory.
* Start the story and let children make another ending, then write the new ending down to use again.
* If a group of children make up their own stories and illustrate them in a book format, use these to make a little classroom library with a storyboard, or use them in a role play corner or as part of a library.

Developing Storyboards for other Activities

Some ideas:

* Use magnetic, Velcro and MDF boards to create other visual effects and develop other areas of the curriculum.
* A Velcro board could have numbers and counters with hook Velcro on the reverse to build up number lines and number bonds or sequence numbers. Use it as a visual aid, or for children to develop number skills.
* Use them to put pictures with different numbers of items in sequence, or to order story sequences.
* Make some name cards so you can use storyboards to construct basic charts such as favourite fruits with children's names above their favourite fruit in a column.
* Use letters on the board to build up cvc words. This allows quick movement of letters as new words are added. Add pictures of objects for even more uses in word recognition. These resources are very valuable for building up vocabulary with children whose first language is not English.
* Put letters, digraphs and pictures on a blank board to make phonic work very visual.
* The boards are good for mind mapping - finding out what children can do or what they know when planning for new topics or units of work.
* When you are moving from one topic to another, use a double sided storyboard so adults and children can start preliminary thinking about the new topic while concluding the previous one.
* Storyboards can be used as day or week planners for groups of children or an individual child. Names and pictures can be added and moved easily, and they can be taken from the board when the activity is completed.

Suppliers

Cardboard boxes
Local supermarkets may have these available. Also contact local industries, as many pack them to be recycled and would not mind you collecting some to re-use in your setting.

Paper and card
Most sorts and sizes will already be available within your setting from educational suppliers, but try local printers who may have offcuts of paper that you can have free.

Plastic storage bags
Small grip seal or zip lock bags are really useful for storage. Get them from your local supermarket or craft shops. They are available in a number of different sizes and are ideal to store pieces for your storyboards.

Lollipop sticks and garden labels
These are available from craft shops and garden centres to stick onto the back of characters if you need to slot them into spaces on the storyboard.

Fabrics
Try local stores or Dickory Dock Designs Tel: 01484 689619
www.dickorydockdesigns.co.uk

Velcro® Products and Velcro® receptive fabric
From Dickory Dock Designs 01484 689619 or
www.dickorydockdesigns.co.uk
A wide range of different colours and types available, including Velcro® photo paper.
Velcro® dots from sewing and craft shops.

Felt
Craft shops and educational suppliers.

Magnetic boards and accessories
Craft suppliers or
Synergy Learning
Tel: 01243 779967 or
www.synergy-group.co.uk

Magnetic paint
Brainstorm
Tel: 01200445113 or
sales@brainstorm.co.uk

Printed Card Pieces to use with storyboards
Sweet Counter
Tel: 07973 152 064 or
www.sweetcounter.co.uk

Autopress Educards 08702403565 or
www.autopresseducation.co.uk

Velcro® boards
Educational suppliers, including Dickory Dock Designs
Tel: 01484 689619 or
www.dickorydockdesigns.co.uk

Storyboard Sets
An extensive range of ready made boards, for all areas of the curriculum, or sets
of pieces, with many including teaching notes are available from
Dickory Dock Designs
Tel: 01484 689619 or
www.dickorydockdesigns.co.uk

A limited range of sets, boards and pieces are also available from some other
educational suppliers.

If you have found this book useful you might also like...

**The Little Book of
Puppets in Stories**
LB43
ISBN 1-905019-33-5
987-1-905019-33-5

**The Little Book of
Storytelling**
LB19
ISBN 1-904187-65-X
987-1-904187-65-3

**The Little Book of
Puppet Making**
LB23
ISBN 1-904187-73-0
978-1-904187-73-8

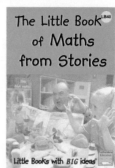

**The Little Book of
Maths from Stories**
LB40
ISBN 1-905019-25-4
987-1-905019-25-0

All available from

Featherstone Education   PO Box 6350

Lutterworth LE17 6ZA

T:0185 888 1212   F:0185 888 1360

on our web site

www.featherstone.uk.com

and from selected
book suppliers